MW01289150

The

Joke Preservation

Society

In our society of political correctness much of our heritage is being lost. Amongst those things that are disappearing from our world is ethnic humor.

Deemed, sometimes rightly so, offensive by the elitists among us, such jokes are now whispered, if spoken at all. Yet they are part of our cultural heritage and history and should not be discarded onto the trash heap of denial.

Thus the JPS is collecting ethnic humor into a series of volumes for future generations to both study and enjoy; to understand where we have come from and better understand where we are going.

Obnoxious Italian Jokes
By
Guido
"Meatballs"
Linguini

Copyright 2016 The Joke
Preservation Society

Cover art courtesy Clipart.com.
Used under license.

ISBN-13:
978-1535060783

ISBN-10:
1535060786

Why is Italy shaped like a boot?
Do you think they could fit all that shit in a tennis shoe?

How does an Italian count his goats?
He just counts the legs, and divides by four.

How do Italian girls shave their legs?
They lie down outside and have someone mow them.

What do you get when you cross an Italian and a Pollack?
A guy who makes you an offer you can't understand.

How do you kill an Italian?
Smash the toilet seat on the back of his head when he is getting a drink.

If Tarzan and Jane were Italian, what would Cheetah be?
The least hairy of the three.

How did they advertise surplus W. W. II Italian rifles for sale?
"Never fired, and only dropped once.

How is the Italian version of Christmas different?
One Mary, one Jesus, and 32 Wise guys.

What did the barber say to the
Italian kid?
Do you want your hair cut or
should I just change the oil.?

Why do Italian men have
mustaches?
So they can look like their mothers.

Why do Puerto Ricans throw their
trash away in clear plastic bags?
So Italians can go window
shopping.

What s an innuendo?
An Italian suppository.

Why are most Italian men named
Tony?
When they got on the boat to
America they stamped To NY
(Tony) on their foreheads.

What do you call an Italian with his
hands in his pocket?
A mute.

Did you hear about the 21 year old
Italian girl who knelt in front of the
statue of Madonna?
She said: "You who conceived
without sin, let me sin without
conceiving!"

Why did the Mafia cross the road?
Forget about it.

What do you get when you cross an Italian and a Jew?
Olive Garden

How can you tell if an Italian is in the Mafia?
His favorite dish is broken leg of lamb.

What do you call an Italian who marries someone Polish?
A social climber.

What do you call an Italian hooker?
A pastatute.

Did you hear about the Italian chef that died?
He pasta way.

What does FIAT stand for?
Fix It Again, Tony!

What do you call a Roman with a cold?
Julius Sneezer

Why are polish jokes so short?
Its so the Italians can understand them.

Why don't Italians have freckles?
Because they slide right off.

What do you call a dodgy neighborhood in Italy?
A Spaghetto.

What's a sure-fire way to know you are Italian?
You are 5'4", can bench 350 lbs, and you still cry when your mother scolds you.

A couple ways to know you're an Italian in the 21st century:
You just tried to enter your password on the microwave.

How do you Impress an Italian Man?
Show up naked, Bring beer

How do you brainwash an Italian?
Give him an enema.

What do you call an Italian with an I.Q. of 180? Sicily.

Did you hear about the Italian
Admiral who wanted to be burred
at sea
when he died?
 Five sailors died digging his grave.

Why is Italian bread so long?
So they can dip it into the sewer.

How can you spot the Italian
junkie?
He's the guy trying to stuff his
crack with pipe.

Hear about the girl that was fired
for eating Italian Sausage?
They fired the Italian guy too.

Hear about the Italian guy that bought his wife a toy poodle?
He accidentally killed it putting the batteries in.

How dumb was the Italian man?
He thought his wife's been in church all night if she comes home with a Gideon Bible.

Why did the Italian jack-off on the football field?
His coach said it was an exhibition game.

Hear about the Italian who went to the dine and had the businessman's lunch?
The businessman was irate.

What did the Italian guy do before going to a cockfight?
He greased his zipper.

A 12-year-old boy walks up to his Italian neighbor and says, "I was looking in your bedroom window last night and I saw you and your wife naked!"
The guy answers, "The joke's on you, Johnny...I wasn't even home last night!"

What did they find when the Berlin Wall came down?
The Italian hide-and-seek champion.

Gross stupidity The population of Italy.

Hear about the Italian twins?
They keep forgetting each other's birthday.

An Italian family is sitting in the living room. The wife turns to the husband and says "Let's send the kids out to
P-L-A-Y so we can go in the bedroom and fuck."

Why did the Italian poker player wear black gloves?
So nobody could see his hand.

How did the Italian lady blow her brains out?
She stepped on her douche bag!

An Italian soldier was confronted by a charging German soldier and a charging Russian soldier. Which did he shoot first, and why?
He shot the German first--business before pleasure.

What's a Italian Bikini consist of?
Two Band-Aids and two corks.

What's lack and crispy and hangs from your ceiling?
A Italian electrician.

Who really assassinated John F. Kennedy?
400 Italian sharpshooters.

A German and an Italian are hunting in the woods. Suddenly a naked woman appears.
German: Boy, I could eat her!
The Italian guy shot her.

What did Jesus say to the Italian people?
"Play dumb 'til I get back."

What do you call a Italian who practices birth control?
Humanitarian.

Why is a Italian scholar and a pound of uncooked hamburger alike?
They are both very rare.

What do you get if you cross a black man and a Italian?
A hit man who misses.

An Italian put odor eaters in his shoes.
He disappeared.

Who wears a dirty white robe and rides a pig?
Lawrence of Italy

Why did the Italian woman stick a candle in her twat?
So her boyfriend could eat by candlelight.

How did the Italian guy die in a pie eating contest?
A cow stepped on his head.

What do you call two Italian women meeting in the shower?
Gorillas in the Mist.

First Italian: "Look! Dead bird!"
The second Italian looks up.

What's an Italian's favorite deodorant?
Raid.

Why did the Italian lose the Indy 500?
He had to stop and ask directions.

The Italian burglar had to break 2 windows.'
One to get in, one to get out.

Then there was the Italian who tried to mug a lawyer and lost $2,000.

What's the difference between a Italian woman and a bowling ball?
You can eat a bowling ball.

What do a Italian woman and a football have in common?
Pigskin.

Why did the Italian refuse to buy Christmas seals?
He didn't know what to feed them.

Did you hear about the Italian who born at home?
His mother saw him and went to the hospital.

Why did the Italian woman stare at her pussy in a mirror?
She was studying for her pap test.

What's the difference between a French girl and an Italian girl?
The French girl turns heads, the Italian girl turns stomachs.

Why did the Italian swim club have a sign that read "ool?"
They didn't want any P in the pool.

Why did the Italian beat his sin after seeing his report card?
He wanted to make him smart.

1st Italian girl: I wonder how long dicks should be sucked?
2nd Italian girl: The same as short ones.

What to ask an Italian with a beautiful woman on his arm?
Where did you get that tattoo?

How do Italians put on their underwear?
Yellow on front. Brown in back.

How do Italian mothers keep their kids from biting their nails?
They make them wear shoes.

How do they make Italian sausage?
From retarded pigs?

Why did the Italian throw away his toilet brush?
He went back to using paper.

Italian Super Bowl: One that doesn't back up.

What did the Italian do when his girlfriend complained about picking his nose?
He picked it himself.

What's the difference between a Italian woman and a chicken?
The chicken is dressed better.

How do waiters serve Italian women?
They put the bowl on the floor.

What do you call a Italian sitting on your lawn?
Fertilizer.

Why did the Italian pee on his wife?
It was their Golden Anniversary.

What did the Italian do when they were out of orange Kool-Aid?
He bought cherry and peed in it.

What's black and brown and looks good on an Italian?
A Doberman.

Why don't they let Italians swim in the lake?
They leave a ring.

Why do Italians wear turtlenecks?
To hide the flea collar.

What's the difference between an elephant and a Italian woman?
20 pounds and the dress.

How does an Italian get into an honest business?
Usually through the skylight.

What did the Italian woman say to her unmarried pregnant daughter?
"Don't worry, maybe it's not yours."

Why is an Italian woman like a hockey team?
They both take showers after three periods

What do most Italian women doe from?
Toxic Sock Syndrome.

How come Italian's don't like Jehovah witnesses?
They don't like any witnesses

How do you shut up an Italian?
Tie their hands behind their back.

Then there was the Italian who thought manual labor was a famous Spanish painter.

What sign is in every Italian restroom?
"Please Don't Eat the Toilet Mint."

Then there was the Italian girl who thought Fucking and Cooking were cities in China.

And the Italian guy who thought Working and Saving were cities in China.

Why don't Italians read Moby Dick?
They think it's about a venereal disease.

How do you get three Italians off the couch?
Jerk one off and the other 2 come.

Did you hear about the queer Italian?
He liked women more than Ssaghetti..

Why don't they kill flies in Italy?
They're the national bird.

Why does an Italian always take a dime along on his dates?
So if he can't come he can call.

"Knock! Knock!"
"Who's there?"
"Italian burglar."

Then there was the Italian actress who went to Hollywood and fucked the writer.

Italian Sex Manual
"In."
"Out"
"Repeat"

How to you know you've been robbed by an Italian burglar?
The garbage's been eaten and the dog is pregnant.

What are the three most difficult years for a Italian?
The second grade.

What do you get when you cross a Italian and a monkey?
Nothing, a monkey is too smart to screw a Italian!

Did you hear about the two bald-headed Italians who put their heads together and made an ass out of themselves?

What do Italians wear to weddings?
Formal bowling shirts.

What does an Italian girl do after she sucks cock?
Spit out the feathers.

What do you call a Italian test tube baby?
Janitor in a Drum.

World's shortest book: Italian Wit and Wisdom.

Italian foreplay: "Brace yourself, woman!"

Then there was the half Italian and half Polish Godfather.
He makes offers you can't understand.

"Dad, can I have five dollars to buy a rat?"
"Here's ten. Go get yourself a nice Italian girl."

Did you hear about the Italian who emigrated to Poland?
He raised the I.Q. of both countries.

What do you get when you cross a Jew and an Italian?
A janitor that thinks he owns the building.

What's the difference between garbage and an Italian girl?
Garage gets picked up.
Why do women slap Italian midgets?
They are always telling them how their hair smells.

Why are Italian women forbidden from swimming in the ocean?
They can't get the smell out of the fish.

How can you tell a Italian woman isn't wearing any underwear?
Dandruff on her shoes.

What does it say on the bottom of a Coke bottle in Italy?
Open other end.

Why do little Italian girls put fish in their underwear?
So they can smell like big Italian girls.

How do you break an Italian's finger?
Hit him on the nose.

What's the difference between a bowling ball and a Italian girl?
You can only fit three fingers in a bowling ball.

Did you hear about the Italian fox that got caught in a trap?
It chewed three of its' legs off before it got free.

What do you get if you cross an Italian and gorilla?
A retarded gorilla.

Why do Italians smell?
So blind people can hate them, too.

How many Italians does it take to rape a girl?
Four. Three to hold her down and one to read the instruction.

What do you do when a 'Italian tank attacks?
Shoot the guy pushing it.

Did you see the Italian submarine with a screen door?
Don't laugh, it keeps the fish out.

How does an Italian practice bondage?
By tying her legs together.

The Italian took his wife to the supermarket when she went into labor.
He heard they had free delivery.

Why did the Italian drive around the block for five hours?
His right turn signal was stuck.

What do you get when you cross an Italian and a Latino?
A Sortarican.

How can you tell the groom at an Italian wedding?
He's the one in a clean bowling shirt.

The Italian helicopter crashed.
The pilot got cold and turned the fan off.

Why do so many Italian names end in "ski?"
They can't spell toboggan.

The Italian mother gave birth to twins?
Now her husband wants to know who the other man was.

Did you hear in the news that a 747 recently crashed in a cemetery in Italy?
The Italian officials have so far retrieved 2000 bodies.

Did you hear about the winner of the Italian beauty contest?
Me neither.

Doctor: Have you had a checkup recently?
Italian woman: No, just a German and a couple Hungarians.

What's the difference between a smart Italian and a unicorn?
Nothing, they're both fictional characters

The Italians just bought 10,000 sceptic tanks.
As soon as they learn how to drive them, they attack!

How does every Italian joke start?
By looking over your shoulder.

4 billion years of evolution and we get Italians?

Did you hear about the million-dollar Italian Lottery?
You win a dollar a year for a million years.

How do you know you're flying over Italy?
When you see toilet paper hanging on the clotheslines.

Why does the new Italian navy have glass bottom boats?
So they can see the old Italian navy.

How many Italians does it take to kidnap a child?
12. One to kidnap the child and the remaining 11 to write a ransom letter.

Then there was the Italian who painted his sundial with luminous paint so he could use it at night.

Why did the Italian couple decide to have only 4 children?
They'd read in the newspaper that one out of every five babies born in the world today is Chinese.

Italians don't act stupid.
It's the real thing.

The Italian housewife wanted a
new dishwasher but her husband
refused to move.

What happened to the Italian
National Library?
Someone stole the book.

The Italian butcher accidently
backed into his meat slicer and got
a little behind in his work.

How do you ruin an Italian party?
Flush the punch bowl.

The Italian accidentally mixed his
Viagra with iron supplement.
Now he can't stop pointing North.

What happens when an Italian doesn't pay his garbage bill?
They stop delivering.

Why did the Italian pour superglue on his nonstick pan?
He wanted to see who right.

How do you confuse an Italian?
Put him in a round room and tell him to piss in the corner.

What happens when a Italian woman has an accident in the kitchen?
Her husband gets it for dinner.

What's the motto of the Italian Solidarity Union?
Every man for himself.

How do Italians practice safe sex?
They never give their real name.

An Italian bursts in on his cheating wife. "What do you think you're doing?"
"See?"" she says to her lover. "I told you he was stupid."

How does an Italian wife know her husband is cheating?
He takes two baths a week.

What did the Italian say when he caught his wife in bed with his best friend?
"Bad dog!"

What do you do if a Italian throws a hand-grenade at you?
Take the pin out and throw it back.

Then there was the Italian that tried some extra strength deodorant.
He disappeared.

Why does the Italian flag have two pieces of Velcro on it?
So that the red and green parts can be detached when any fighting starts.

How do you stop an Italian army on horseback?
Turn off the carousel.

Italian women have a complexion like a peach.
Yellow and fuzzy.

Why did the Italian woman spend 5 hours in the beauty parlor?
She was getting an estimate.

Why wasn't Christ born in Italy?
Because they couldn't find three wise men and a virgin.

How do you make an Italian laugh on Monday?
Tell him a joke on Friday.

What is one idea that never got off the ground?
An Italian Air Force.

How do you sink an Italian battleship?
Put it in water.

How do you get a one-armed Italian out of a tree?
Wave to him.

A Mafia Godfather finds out that his bookkeeper has screwed him for ten million bucks.
This bookkeeper is deaf.
It was considered an occupational benefit, and why he got the job in the first place, since it was assumed that a deaf bookkeeper would not be able to hear anything he'd ever have to testify about in court.
When the Godfather goes to shakedown the bookkeeper about his missing $10 million bucks, he brings along his attorney, who knows sign language.
The Godfather asks the bookkeeper: "Where is the 10

million bucks you embezzled from me?"

The attorney, using sign language, asks the bookkeeper where the 10 million dollars is hidden.

The bookkeeper signs back:

"I don't know what you are talking about.

"The attorney tells the Godfather: "He says he doesn't know what you're talking about."

That's when the Godfather pulls out a 9 mm pistol, puts it to the bookkeeper's temple, cocks it, and says: "Ask him again!"

The attorney signs to the underling: "He'll kill you for sure if you don't tell him!"

The bookkeeper signs back: "OK! You win! The money is in a brown briefcase, buried behind the shed in my cousin Enzo's backyard in Queens!"

The Godfather asks the attorney: "Well, what'd he say?"

The attorney replies: "He says you don't have the balls to pull the trigger."

At St. Peter's Catholic Church in Toronto, they have weekly husbands' marriage seminars.

At the session last week, the priest asked Giuseppe, who said he was approaching his 50th wedding anniversary, to take a few minutes and share some insight into how he had managed to stay married to the same woman all these years.

Giuseppe replied to the assembled husbands,'Wella, I'va tried to treat her nicea, spenda da money on her,

but besta of all is, I tooka her to Italy for the 25th anniversary!'
The priest responded,'Giuseppe, you are an amazing inspiration to all the husbands here! Please tell us now what you are planning for your wife for your 50th anniversary?'
Giuseppe proudly replied, "I gonna go pick her up "

Big Lorenzo, an Italian fella, is bragging to his friends about his sons:
"I'ma so prouda my oldest son. He maka fifty thousand dollar evra year. Hesa Engineer!"
"I even more prouda ma second son. He maka five hundred thousand dollar a year. Hesa Doctor!"
"But, I'ma da proudest a ma

youngest son. He maka Five million dollar a year. Hesa Sports Mechanic!"
Paolo, his friend asks: "What's a Sports Mechanic?"
Lorenzo replies: "Wella, he can fixa everytin. He fixa da horseraces, he fixa da boxin matcha..."

Two Italian bowling teams charter a double-decker bus to go to Atlantic City for the weekend.
One team is in the bottom of the bus, and the other team is in the top of the bus.
The team down below is whooping it up when one of them realizes he doesn't hear anything from the top.
He walks up the stairs, and here are all the guys from the second team

clutching the seats in front of them with white knuckles, scared to death.

He says, "What the heck's goin' on? We're down here havin' a grand old time."

One of the guys from the second team says, "Yeah, but you guys've got a driver."

Emma, who was on a sinking ship, was thinking? I.m too young to die.? Then, she yelled at the people around? Well, if I'm going to die, I want my last minutes on earth to be memorable! Is there anyone on this ship who can make me feel like a woman?

For a moment, there was silence.

No response came for a while.

Then an Italian man stood up. He

was gorgeous, tall, well built, with dark brown hair and hazel eyes. He started to walk slowly up the aisle, unbuttoning his shirt...one button at a time. No one moved. He removed his shirt. Muscles rippled across his chest...

She gasps...

He whispers...

Iron this, and get me something to eat.

An old Italian lived alone in New Jersey.

He wanted to plant his annual tomato garden, but it was very difficult work, as the ground was hard.

His only son, Vincent, who used to help him, was in prison.

The old man wrote a letter to his

son and described his predicament:

Dear Vincent,
I am feeling pretty sad, because it looks like I won't be able to plant my tomato garden this year. I'm just getting too old to be digging up a garden plot. I know if you were here my troubles would be over... I know you would be happy to dig the plot for me, like in the old days.
Love, Papa
A few days later he received a letter from his son.
Dear Pop,
Don't dig up that garden. That's where the bodies are buried.
Love, Vinnie
At 4 a.m. the next morning, FBI agents and local police arrived and dug up the entire area without

finding any bodies. They apologized to the old man and left. That same day the old man received another letter from his son.

Dear Pop,

Go ahead and plant the tomatoes now. That's the best I could do under the circumstances.

Love, Vinnie

Mrs. Ravioli comes to visit her son Anthony for dinner. He lives with a female roommate, Maria. During the course of the meal, his mother couldn't help but notice how pretty Anthony's roommate is. Over the course of the evening, while watching the two interact, she started to wonder if there was more between Anthony and his roommate than met the eye.

Reading his mom's thoughts, Anthony volunteered, "I know what you must be thinking, but I assure you, Maria and I are just roommates."

About a week later, Maria came to Anthony saying, "Ever since your mother came to dinner, I've been unable to find the silver sugar bowl. You don't suppose she took it, do you?"

"Well, I doubt it, but I'll email her, just to be sure." So he sat down and wrote an email:

Dear Mama,

I'm not saying that you "did" take the sugar bowl from my house; I'm not saying that you "did not" take it. But the fact remains that it has

been missing ever since you were
here for dinner.
Your Loving Son
Anthony
Several days later, Anthony
received a response email from his
Mama which read:
Dear son,
I'm not saying that you "do" sleep
with Maria, and I'm not saying that
you "do not" sleep with her. But the
fact remains that if she was
sleeping in her OWN bed, she
would have found the sugar bowl
by now.
Your Loving Mama

A bus stops and two Italian men get on. They sit down and engage in an animated conversation. The lady sitting behind them ignores them at first, but her attention is galvanized when she hears one of the men say the following..."Emma come first.
Den I come.
Den two asses come together.
I come once-a-more.
Two asses, they come together again.
I come again and pee twice.
Then I come one lasta time."
"You foul-mouthed swine, " retorted the lady indignantly. "In this country we don't talk about our sex lives in public! "Hey, coola down lady," said the man/ "Who talkin' abouta sexa? I'm a justa

tellin' my frienda how to spella Mississippi."

Bless me Father, for I have sinned.
I have been with a loose woman.
The priest asks, Is that you, little Johnny Parisi?
Yes, Father, it is.
And who was the woman you were with?
I can't tell you, Father.
I don't want to ruin her reputation.
Well, Johnny, I'm sure to find out her name sooner or later, so you may as well tell me now.
Was it Tina Minetti?
I cannot say.
Was it Teresa Volpe?
I'll never tell.
Was it Nina Capelli?
I'm sorry, but I cannot name her.

Was it Cathy Piriano?
My lips are sealed.
Was it Rosa Di Angelo, then?
Please, Father, I cannot tell you.
The priest sighs in frustration.
You're very tight lipped, Johnny
Parisi, and I admire that.
But you've sinned and have to
atone.
You cannot be an altar boy now for
4 months.
Now you go and behave yourself.
Johnny walks back to his pew, and
his friend Nino slides over and
whispers, What'd you get?
Four months' vacation and five
good leads.

HEAVEN is where:
The police are British
The chefs Italian
The mechanics are German
The lovers are French
and it's all organized by the Swiss

HELL is where:
The police are German
The chefs are British
The mechanics are French
The lovers are Swiss
and it's all organized by the
Italians!!

A man was leaving a 7-11 with his
morning coffee and newspaper
when he noticed a most unusual
funeral procession approaching the
nearby cemetery.
A long black hearse was followed

by a second long black hearse about 50 feet behind. Behind the second hearse was a solitary Italian guy walking a pit bull on a leash. Behind him were 200 men walking single file. The guy couldn't stand the curiosity. He respectfully approached the Italian walking the dog and said "Sir, I know now is a bad time to disturb you, but I've never seen a funeral like this. Whose funeral is it?"

The Italian replied: "Well, that first hearse is for my wife."

"What happened to her?" The man replied: "My dog attacked and killed her."

He inquired further: "Well, who is in the second hearse?"

The Italian answered, "My mother-in-law. She was trying to help my

wife when the dog turned on her."
A poignant and thoughtful moment of silence passes between the two men.
"Sir, could I borrow that dog?"
"Get in line."

An American attorney had just finished a guest lecture at a law school in Italy when an Italian lawyer approached him and asked, "Is it true that a person can fall down on a sidewalk in your county and then sue the landowners for lots of money?"
Told that it was true, the lawyer turned to his partner and started speaking rapidly in Italian. When they stopped, the American attorney asked if they wanted to go to America to practice law.

"No, no," one replied. "We want to go to America and fall down on sidewalks."

A Russian, an Italian and an Irishman got out of work and were deciding where to go for a drink. The Irishman said "Let's all go to O'Learys. With every third round, the bartender will give each of us a free Guiness."
The Russian said "That sounds good, but if we go to Gouvstof's with every third round they bring a free bottle of vodka to the table."
 The Italian said "That sounds fine but if we go to Baldini's we drink for free all night and then go out into the parking lot and get laid."

"That sounds to good to be true!" the Irishman exclaimed. "Have you actually been there?"
"No," the Italian replied, "but my wife goes there all the time.

+An English guy is driving with a Italian guy as his passenger, when he decides to pull over because he suspects that his turn signal may not be working. He asks the Italian guy if he doesn't mind stepping out of the car to check the lights while he tests them. The Italian guy steps out and stands in front of the car. The English guy turns on the turn signal and asks, "Is it working?"
 To which the Italian guy responds, "Yes, it's working...No, it's not working...Yes, it's working...No, it's not working...."

Two Italian guys are driving through Texas when they get pulled over by a state trooper. The trooper walks up and taps on the window with his nightstick.

The driver rolls down the window, and the trooper smacks him in the head with the stick. The driver says, "Why'd you do that?

The trooper says, "You're in Texas, son. When I pull you over, you'll have your license ready."

Driver says, "I'm sorry, officer, I'm not from around here."

The trooper runs a check on the guy's license, and he's clean. He gives the guy his license back and walks around to the passenger side and taps on the window. The passenger rolls his window down, and the trooper smacks him with

the nightstick.
The passenger says, "What'd you do that for?"
The cop says, "Just making your wishes come true."
The passenger says, "Huh?"
The cop says, "I know that two miles down the road you're gonna say, 'I wish that guy would've tried that crap with me!

A Greek and Italian were sitting in a Starbuck's one day discussing who had the superior culture.
Over triple lattes the Greek guy says, "Well, we have the Parthenon."
Arching his eyebrows, the Italian replies, "We have the Coliseum."
The Greek retorts, "We Greeks gave birth to advanced

mathematics."
The Italian, nodding agreement, says, "But we built the Roman Empire."
And so it goes on until the Greek comes up with what he thinks will end the discussion.
With a flourish of finality he says, "We invented sex!"
The Italian replies, "That is true, but it was the Italians who introduced it to women!

The young Italian lad looked into his girlfriend's eyes and said, "I really love you. Would you let me change your name to mine?"
"Oh, yes, that would be wonderful!"
From that day on, he called her Vinnie.

Two Italians, Luigi and Antonio, met on the street. "Hey, Antonio," said Luigi, "Where you been for the past two weeks? No one seen you around."

"Dona talka to me, Luigi," replied Antonio. "I been inna jail."

"Jail!" exclaimed Luigi. "What for you been in jail?"

"Wella, Luigi," Antonio said, "I was lying onna dis beach, and the cops come, arrest me and throw me inna jail."

"But dey dona throw you in jail just for lying onna da beach!", Luigi countered.

"Yeah, but dis beach was screamin' and akickin' and ayellin'!"

Francis and Isabella were having their usual battle of the sexes. "Italian men are all stupid," screamed Isabella
"Oh, yeah?" yelled her husband. "I'll have you know it was an Italian man who invented the toilet seat!" "And I'll have you know," said his wife, "it was an Italian woman who thought of putting a hole in it!"

Vinny and Sal are out in the woods hunting. Suddenly Sal grabs his chest and falls to the ground. He doesn't seem to be breathing, his eyes are rolled back in his head. Vinny whips out his cell phone and dials 911.
He gasps to the operator: 'I think Sal is dead! What should I do?'
The operator, in a calm soothing

voice says: 'Just take it easy and follow my instructions:
'First, let's make sure he's dead.'
There is a long silence …….and then a shot is heard.
Vinny's voice comes back on the line:
"Okay… now what?'

Lulgi was walking along a Boulevard, involved in a prayer.
He asked God for one wish.
Suddenly, the sky clouded above his head and in a booming voice, God said, "Because you have had the faith to ask, I will grant you one wish."
The man said, "Build a bridge to Italy, so I can drive over anytime I want to."
God was in awkward situation...
God said, "Your request is very

materialistic.

Think of the logistics of that kind of undertaking.

All the technology needed to reach the bottom of the ocean!

The concrete and steel it would take!

I can do it, but it is hard for me to justify your desire for worldly things.

Think for some time and ask another wish."

Luigi thought for a while and then said, "God, I have been married and divorced three times.

All of my wives said that I am uncaring and insensitive.

Here is my wish: I would like to know how to make an Italian woman happy."

The God went in heavy thought

mode, and said, "OK, son, you want two lanes or four on that bridge?"

After returning from his honeymoon in Florida with his new bride, Virginia, Luigi stopped in his New York neighborhood barbershop to say hello to his friends.
Giovanni said, "Hey, Luigi. How was'a da treep?"
Luigi said, "Ever'thing was'a perfect except for da train'a ride down."
"What'a you mean, Luigi?" asked Giovanni.
"Well, we board'a da train at Grand Central'a Station. My beautiful'a Virginia had packed a big'a basket a food with vino and cigars for'a me, and'a we were looking

'aforward to da trip. All was OK until we got'a hungry and opened up'a da lunch'a basket.

"The conductor came by, wagged his'a finger at us and'a say, 'No eat in dese'a car. Must'a use'a dining car.'

"So, me and my beautiful'a Virginia, we go to dining car, eat a big'a lunch and begin to open'a bottle of vino.

Conductor come again, wag his'a finger and say, 'No drink'a in dese'a car. Must'a use'a club'a car.'

"So we go to club'a car. While'a drinking vino, I start to light'a my big'a cigar.

The conductor, he wag'a his finger again and say, 'No smoke'a in dese'a car. Must'a go to smoker car.'

"We go to smoker car and I smoke'a my cigar.
Later, my beautiful Virginia and I, we go to sleeper car and'a go to bed.
And then here come'a the conductor, he come'a through the car yelling, 'NO-FOLK'A, VIRGINIA!'"

This Italian bloke had never played golf before and so asked for some tips before starting the game. An American player decided to teach the Italian the proper way to putt a golf ball. The American said, "You take this stick and hit the balls so that they roll into the hole". The American putted away and sank the ball from 20 feet in a single stroke. The Italian replied, "In America, you leave your sticka outta and a putta your balls in da hole, but in Italia, we put our sticka inna da hole and leave our balls out"!

An old Italian woman is riding the elevator in a very lavish New York City Office Building. A young and beautiful woman gets into the elevator and smelling like expensive perfume turns to the old Italian woman and says arrogantly, "Giorgio Beverly Hills, $100 an ounce!"
The next young and beautiful woman gets on the elevator and also very arrogantly turns to the old Italian woman and says, "Chanel No. 5, $150 an ounce!"
About three floors later, the old Italian woman has reached her destiny and is about to get off the

elevator. Before she leaves, looks both beautiful women in the eye, she bends over, and passes gas... "Broccoli - 49 cents a pound."

A French couple, an Irish couple, and a Italian couple were having dinner together. The Frenchman says to his wife, "Pass me the sugar, sugar."
Not to be outdone, the Irishman asks his wife, "Could you pass me the honey, honey?"
Much impressed by these clever endearments, the Italians leans over to his wife and says, "Pass the pork, pig."

An Italian man immigrates to America. He starts sweeping floors in a pizzeria, and after 15 years works his way up to owning a small chain of pizzerias. He decides to have his own house designed and built for him. And it is going to have everything!

One day he is talking to the contractor and said, "Makea you sure you puta plenty da halo statues inna da house. I wanna hava lotsa da halo statues. One inna every room, even da bathroom."

The contractor, realizing his client must be a very religious person, carefully plans a niche in every room, and personally searches for the perfect statue for each niche.

Finally, the house is finished. The Italian man walks through his new home for the first time.

The contractor points out all the features, and finally the Italian man

said, "But wherea are alluh myhalo statues?
I wanna lotsa halo statues!" And the contractor points to the niches and said, "I put a statue in every room, like you asked."
The Italian replies, "No, no, no! I donna no wanna nonea daSaintas. I wanna da Halo Statues!
You knowa da Halo Statues? Deya ring anda you picka dem up, anna you say, halo 'stat you?"

An Italian grandmother is giving directions to her grown grandson who is coming to visit with his wife. "You comma to de front door of the apartmenta. I am inna apartmenta 301. There issa bigga panel at the front door. With you elbow, pusha button 301. I will

buzza you in. Come inside, the elevator is on the right. Get in and with you elbow , pusha 3. When you get out, I'mma on the left. With you elbow, hit my doorbell."
"Grandma, that sounds easy, but, why am I hitting all these buttons with my elbow?
"What . . . . You coming empty handed?"

Five Englishmen in an Audi Quattro arrive at the Italian border. The Italian customer agent stops them and tells them:
"Itsa illegal to putta fiva people ina Quattro."
"What do you mean it's illegal?" asked the Englishmen.
"Quattro means four," replies the Italian official.

"Quattro is just the name of the automobile,"
The Englishman says, not believing what he is hearing.
"Look at the papers: this car is designed to carry 5 persons."
"You can'ta pulla thata one ona me," replies the Italian customs agent.
"Quattro means four. You hava fiva people ina your car and you are therefore breakin'a the law".
The Englishman replies angrily, "You idiot! Call your supervisor over We want to speak to someone with more intelligence!"
"Sorry," responds the Italian official, "he can'ta come".
"He's a busy with two guys in a Uno".

Joey prepared a pasta dish for a dinner party he was giving. In his haste, however, he forgot to refrigerate the spaghetti sauce, and it sat on the counter all day. He was worried about spoilage, but it was too late to cook up another batch. He called the local Poison Control Center and voiced his concern. They advised Stumpy to boil the sauce again.

That night, the phone rang during dinner, and a guest volunteered to answer it. Joey's face dropped as the guest called out, "It's the Poison Control Center. They want to know how the spaghetti sauce turned out."

Giuseppe walks into work, and he says, "Ey, Tony! You know who's-

a George Washington?"
Tony says, "No, Giuseppe, who's-a
George Washington?"
He says, "Hah! George-a
Washington's the first-a President
of-a United States.
I'm-a go to night school, learn all
about-a United States, and become-
a U.S.-a citizen."
A couple of days later, Giuseppe
walks into work and says."Ey,
Tony, you know who's-a Abraham
Lincoln?"
Tony says, "No, Giuseppe, who's-a
Abraham Lincoln?"
He says, "Hah! Abraham-a Lincoln
is-a sixteenth President of-a the
United States. I'm-a go to night
school, learn all about-a United
States, and become-a U.S.-a
citizen."

A guy in the back of the shop yells, "Yo, Giuseppe . . . you know who Fishlips Lorenzo is?"

He says, "No. Who's-a Fishlips Lorenzo is?"

The guy yells, "That's the guy who's seein' your wife while you're in night school."

A Italian is looking to buy a saw to cut down some trees in his back yard. He goes to a chainsaw shop and asks about various chainsaws.

The dealer tells him, "Look, I have a lot of models, but why don't you save yourself a lot of time and aggravation and get the top-of-the-line model. This chainsaw will cut a hundred cords of wood for you in

one day."
So the Italian takes the chainsaw
home and begins working
on the trees. After cutting for
several hours and only
cutting two cords, he decides to
quit. He thinks there
is something wrong with the
chainsaw.
"How can I cut for hours and only
cut two cords?",
the Italian asks himself. "I will
begin first thing in the
morning and cut all day", the
Italian tells himself. So,
the next morning the Italian gets up
at 4 in the morning
and cuts, and cuts, and cuts till
nightfall, and he
only manages to cut five cords.

The Italian is convinced this is a bad saw. "The dealer told me it would cut one hundred cords of wood in a day, no problem. I will take this saw back to the dealer", the Italian says to himself. The very next day the Italian brings the saw back to the dealer and explains the problem. The dealer, baffled by the Italian's claim, removes the chainsaw from the case. The dealer says, "Huh, it looks fine." Then the dealer starts the chainsaw, to which the Italian responds, "What's that noise?"

Luigi and Paulo were fishing in the Mediterranean Sea one sunny day

when a World War II mine came floating along. On seeing this round, spikey object coming nearer and nearer, Luigi shouts at his friend " Hey Paulo, it's a mine, it's a mine!"
Paulo replies " O.K. Luigi, you can-a have it!!! "

Sophie just got married, and being a traditional Italian was still a virgin. On her wedding night, staying at her mother's house, she was nervous. But mother reassured her. "Don't worry, Sophie. Luca's a good man. Go upstairs, and he'll take care of you."
So up she went. When she got upstairs, Luca took off his shirt and exposed his hairy chest. Sophie ran downstairs to her mother and says,

"Mama, Mama, Luca's got a big hairy chest." "Don't worry, Sophie", says the mother, "All good men have hairy chests. Go upstairs. He'll take good care of you."
So, up she went again. When she got up in the bedroom, Luca took off his pants exposing his hairy legs. Again Sophie ran downstairs to her mother. "Mama, Mama, Luca took off his pants, and he's got hairy legs!"
"Don't worry. All good men have hairy legs. Luca's a good man. Go upstairs, and he'll take good care of you." So, up she went again. When she got up there, Luca took off his socks, and on his left foot he was missing three toes.

When Sophie saw this, she ran downstairs. "Mama, Mama, Luca's got a foot and a half!"
"Stay here and stir the pasta", says the mother. "This is a job for Mama!"

At the World Women's Conference, the first speaker from England stood up:
"At last year's conference we spoke about being more assertive with our husbands. Well after the conference I went home and told my husband that I would no longer cook for him and that he would have to do it himself. After the first day I saw nothing. After the second day I saw nothing. But after the third day I saw that he had cooked a wonderful roast lamb."

The crowd cheered.

The second speaker from America stood up:

"After last year's conference I went home and told my husband that I would no longer do his laundry and that he would have to do it himself. After the first day I saw nothing. After the second day I saw nothing. But after the third day I saw that he had done not only his own washing but my washing as well."

The crowd cheered.

The third speaker from Italy stood up:

"After last year's conference I went home and told my husband that I would no longer do his shopping and that he would have to do it himself. After the first day I saw nothing. After the second day I saw nothing. But after the third day I could see a little bit out of my left eye."

A guy goes into a store and tells the clerk, "I'd like some Italian sausage."
The clerk looks at him and says, "Are you Italian?"
The guy, clearly offended, says, "Well, yes I am. But let me ask you something." If I had asked for Polish sausage would you ask me if I was Polish? Or if I had asked for German bratwurst, would you ask me if I was German? Or if I asked for a kosher hot dog would you ask me if I was Jewish? Or if I had asked for a taco would you ask if I was Mexican? Would ya, huh? Would ya?"

The clerk says, "Well, no."
With deep self-righteous indignation, the guy says, "Well, all right then, why did you ask me if I'm Italian just because I ask for Italian sausage?"
The clerk replies, "Because this is Home Depot."

Vinny Calabrese, right off the boat from Italy, was excited about being accepted at Harvard University. On his first day on campus, he was walking around looking for the library. He saw an upperclassman standing by a tree, walked up to him and said, "Hey piasano, coulda you tella me where isa da library at?"
The upperclassman said, "Here at Harvard we never end sentences

with a preposition. Would you like to rephrase that question?"
"OK, fora you, no problem, Piasano," said the Italian. "Tella me, do you know where isa da library at, youa asshole?"

Two Italians walk into the post office and the first thing that catches their eye is a bunch of "Wanted" posters, in particular a shot of a mean-looking black guy beneath a banner that says "Wanted for Rape."
"You know," said one Italian to his friend, "they get all the good jobs."

A Italian businessman on his deathbed called his good friend and said, "Luigi, I want you to promise me that when I die you will have my remains cremated."

"And what," his friend asked, "do you want me to do with your ashes?"

The businessman said, "Just put them in an envelope and mail them to the IRS...and write on the envelope, 'Now you have everything.'"

A big semi on the interstate pulls over and picks up a pretty young Italian hitchhiker.

While they are driving, the trucker, a serious CB addict, is showing off an enormous new CB radio implanted in his dashboard.

"That's the best CB radio ever made," he explains to the bug-eyed girl. "You can talk anywhere in the world with it."

"No kidding," she gasps. "Boy, I'd really love to talk to my mother in Italy."

"Oh, yeah?"

"I would give anything to talk to my mother in Italy."

"Anything?" he asks.

"Anything," she assures him.

"Well, maybe we can work something out," he leers, pulling his cock, by this time erect, out of his pants.

The girl leans over, bends down, and says loudly, "Hello, Mom!"

Once there was a man that came from Italy to America, He couldn't speak English so he went to choir and learned how to say "Me me me me me me."

Then he went to the store and saw a little girl say "He stole my dolly" And on his way home he went to get meat from the butcher and learned how to say "Big butcher knife big butcher knife."

Then he went home and watched an air freshener commercial and learned how to say "Plug it in Plug it in."

Then he went to the store and there was a murder the police said "Who killed this man?"

The Italain said "Me me me me me me."

The police said "Why did you kill him?"

And the man said "He stole my dolly."

The police man said "What did you kill him with?"

The man said "Big butcher knife big butcher knife."
Then they took him to jail and sentenced him to death. The police man said "any last words?" And the Italian said "Plug it in plug it in."

Two Italians are building a house. One of them is putting on the siding. He picks up a nail, hammers it in. Picks up another nail, throws it away. Picks up a nail, hammers it in. Picks up another, throws it away. This goes on for a while, and finally his friend comes over and asks him why he is throwing half of the nails away. He replies, "Those ones were pointed on the wrong end."

His Italian friend gets exasperated and says "You idiot, those are for the other side of the house!"

A Italian and a Jew were in a bar watching TV when the late-night news came on. The lead story showed a berserk woman poised on a window ledge elevcn stories up. "I'll bet you a hundred bucks she won't jump," said the Italian to the Jew.
"Deal," agreed the Jew, sticking out his hand a few minutes later when the woman plunged to a gory death. The Italian sadly forked over the money, only to look up in surprise as the other fellow tugged on his sleeve and offered him his money back. "You won it fair and square," he said, shaking his head.

"Not really," admitted the Jewish guy. "I saw it all happen on the six o'clock news."

"Me too," said the Italian, "but I never thought she'd do it again at eleven."

The three little pigs... You know the story. The big bad wolf starts in 'huffing and puffing' on the house made of straw, so that little pig runs over to his brother's place made of sticks. The wolf starts to blow the stick house down, so they run over to join their third brother in the brick house. The wolf meanwhile starts huffing and puffing at the brick house. The windows rattle, the door shakes. The third pig picks up his phone and makes a call. Pretty soon a big black Lincoln

Continental pulls up and out steps 2 really rough looking pigs. Wearing black fedora hats, they are dressed all in black, except for white ties. They also have machine guns, and they quickly make mincemeat out of the wolf.

"Who the hell are they?" ask the first two pigs.

Replies the third pig, "They're our neighbors, the Guinea pigs!

Two Italians emigrated to America. On their first day in New York City, they spotted a hot dog vendor in the street.

"Do they eat dogs in America?" one asked the other.

"I dunno."

"Well, we're going to live here, so we might as well learn to do as they

do." So they each bought a hot dog wrapped up and sat down to eat them on a nearby park bench.
One Italian looked at his hot dog, then over at the other Italian and asked, "What part did you get?"

Old Antonio, is a tight ass with his money, reckons he is going to take all his money with him when he dies. Maria, his good wife of many years, protests profusely, "Antonio, you cannota take da money, what about me and da children?"
Antonio replies: "Screw you bitch, it's my money and I earned it!"
So duly on the day of Antonio's funeral, Maria and the kids are crying over papa's coffin, when one of the children speaks up:

"Momma you didn't give pappa the money did you?"

Maria replied: "Yes I gave the dead bastard his fucking money, it's in a check, let's see him cash that!"

John, a Italian, goes into an outhouse and sees his buddy, Stash, with a long stick stirring the contents of one of the receptacles. "What the hell are you doing, Stash" asks John.

"I'm trying to get my jacket out of the hole, it fell in while I was taking a crap at the other hole."

"Are you crazy?" asks John. "It's going to be covered with shit. You won't be able to wear it".

"I know," says Stash, "I'm not that stupid. I just wanted to get my sandwich out of the pocket so I could eat my lunch."

These two Italian guys rent a boat and go fishing on a lake. They are amazed at the number of fish that they caught that day, so one says to the other, "We'll have to come back here tomorrow!"
The other asks, "But how will we remember where this spot is?"
The first guy then takes a can of spray paint, paints an X on the bottom of the boat, and says, "We'll just look for this X tomorrow."
The other guy says, "You idiot! How do you know we'll get the same boat?"

You know how American ships' names begin with "USS", which stands for "United States Service." Then there are British ships, which names begin with "HMS" for "Her Majesty's Service."
So why do Italian ships' names start with "AMB"? "Att-sa My Boat!

An Englishman, a Frenchman and a Italian were captured by the Germans and thrown into prison. However, the guard was rather kind towards them, and said, "I am going to lock you away for five years,
but I'll let you have anything you want now before I lock you away." The Englishman says, "I'll have five years' supply of beer!"

His wish is granted, and they lock him away with his beer.

The Frenchman says, "I'll have five years' supply of brandy!"

His wish is granted, and they lock him away with his brandy.

The Italian says, "I'll have five years' supply of cigarettes!"

His wish is granted, and they lock him away with his cigarettes.

Five years later, the Germans come to release their prisoners. First, they release the Englishman, who staggers out totally drunk. Then, they release the Frenchman, who also rolls out rather inebriated. Then, they release the Italian, who comes out and says, "Has anyone got a light?"

An Italian man immigrates to the United States of America and moves in with some distant relatives in New Jersey. They tell him he should apply for citizenship and they will help him study for the test. They go over all the U.S. history from the Revolutionary war to present day.

Finally, he feels he has enough knowledge to pass the test so he sets an appointment.

He walks into the testing room and the agent giving the test thought he would have a bit of fun, so he said to the man "We have a very simple test for you today. If you can use three English words in one sentence, you will be granted citizenship! The words are green, pink and yellow.

The Italian man thought for several minutes and finally said "O.K., I think I can do that"
Then he said "I hearda the telephone go green, green, green, so I pink it uppa and I say yellow - who is this."

There were two Indians and a Italian fellow walking along together in the desert, when, all of a sudden, one of the Indians took off and ran up this hill to the mouth of a cave. He stopped and hollered into the cave... "Woooooo! Woooooo! Woooooo!" and then listened very closely until he heard the answer... "Woooooo! Woooooo! Woooooo!" He then tore off his clothes and ran in to the cave.

The Italian fellow was puzzled and asked the other Indian what that was all about, was that Indian goofy or something?

"No", said the other Indian. "It is mating time for us Indians and when you see a cave and holler, "Woooooo! Woooooo! Woooooo!", and get an answer back, that means that she is in there waiting for you. Well, just about that time, the other Indian saw another cave. He took off and ran up to the cave, then stopped and hollered, "Woooooo! Woooooo! Woooooo!" When he heard the return, "Woooooo! Woooooo! Woooooo!", off came the clothes and into the cave he went.

The Italian guy starts running around the desert... looking for a cave to find these women that the Indians had talked about. All of a sudden, he looked up and saw this great big cave. As he looked in amazement, he was thinking, Man! Look at the size of that cave! It's bigger than the ones that those Indians found. There must really be something really great in this cave!"

Well... he took off up the hill at a super fast speed with his hopes of ecstasy and grandeur. He got in front of the cave and hollered, "Woooooo! Woooooo! Woooooo!" He was just tickled all over when he heard the answering call of,"WOOOOOOOOO! WOOOOOOOOO!! WOOOOOOOOO!!! Off came his clothes and, with a big smile on his

face, he raced into the cave.
The next day, in the newspaper, the headlines read, "NAKED ITALIAN RUN OVER BY FREIGHT TRAIN!"

An Italian man was having an affair with his neighbor. Shortly afterward, she told him that she was pregnant. Not wanting his wife to know, he gave the neighbor a sum of money and asked her to go to Italy and have the baby there. "But how will I let you know the baby is born?" she asked. He replied, " Just send me a postcard and write "spaghetti" on the back. I'll take care of expenses."
The husband replies, "Yes, I do! You have been asking me that every day since the month after we

got married but you have never asked me if I love spaghetti".

Not knowing what else to do, the neighbor took the money and flew to Italy.

Six months went by, and then one day the Italian man's wife called him at the office and said, "Dear, you received a very strange postcard in the mail today from Europe, and I don't understand what it means." The Italian man said, "Just wait until I get home and I will explain it to you."

Later that evening the Italian man came home, read the postcard, and fell to the floor with a heart attack. Paramedics rushed him to the hospital emergency room. The head medic stayed back to comfort the wife. He asked what trauma had precipitated the cardiac arrest. So the wife picked told the medic that she handed her husband a post card he received from Italy. The card said, "Spaghetti, Spaghetti, Spaghetti, Spaghetti - Two with sausage and meatballs; two without."

Three men are traveling in the Amazon, a German, an American, and a Italian, and they get captured by some Amazons. The head of the tribe says to the German, "What do you want on your back for your whipping?"
The German responds, "I will take oil!" So they put oil on his back, and a large Amazon whips him 10 times. When he is finished the

German has these huge welts on his back, and he can hardly move.
The Amazons haul the German away, and say to the Italian, "What do you want on your back?" "I will take nothing!" says the Italian, and he stands there straight and takes his 10 lashings without a single flinch.
"What will you take on your back?" the Amazons ask the American.
He responds, "I'll take the Italian!"

An Italian man wants to get married but he has trouble choosing among three Italian women. He gives each Italian woman a present of $500 and asks them to spend the money anyway they wish.
The first lady does a total makeover. She goes to a fancy

beauty salon, gets her hair done, new makeup; buys several new outfits and dresses up very nicely for the man. She tells him that she has done this to be more attractive for him because she loves him so much. The Italian man was very impressed.

The second goes shopping to buy the Italian man gifts. She gets him a new Italian suit, some new shoes for his Italian suit, and an expensive Italian tie. As she presents these gifts, she tells him that she has spent all the money on him because she loves him so much. Again, the Italian man is impressed.

The third Italian woman invests the money in the stock market. She earns several times the $500. She gives him back his $500 and reinvests the remainder in a joint account. She tells him that she wants to save for their future because she loves him so much. Obviously, the Italian man was impressed.

The man thought for a long time about what each woman had done with the money he'd given her. Then he married the one with the biggest breasts.

Two Italians are talking about their friend who immigrated to America. "Did you hear about Luigi? He opened up a jewelery store after just one year in America!"
"How did he do That?"
"With a crowbar."

A dietitian was once addressing a large audience at a health seminar. "The material we call food that we put into our stomachs today is enough to have killed most of us sitting here, years ago.

Red meat is awful. Soft drinks erode your stomach lining. Chinese food is loaded with MSG. Macaroni is fattening, Vegetables can be disastrous, and none of us realizes the long-term harm caused by the germs in our drinking water. But there is one thing that is the most dangerous of all and we all have eaten, or will eat it at one point in our lives. Can anyone here tell me what food produces the most long term damage to us even years after eating it?"

A 75-year-old Italian man in the front row stood up and said, "It'sa d' Weddinga cake"

Man goes to a whore house. The Madam is out of women but, since the guy is Italian she thinks she can get away with a blow up doll and he will never know the difference. Being a bit nervous because she has never tried this one before, The Madam waits outside the door. The Italian comes out in five minutes. "How was it?", says the Madam. "I don't know," says the Italian, "I bit her on the tit and she farted and flew out the window!"

In America the late night news used to broadcast this message: "It's 11 o'clock do you know where your children are?"

In England they say "It's 11 o'clock do you know where your wife is?"

In France they say "It's 11 o'clock do you know where your husband is?"

In Italy they say "It's 11 o'clock do you know what time it is?"

A Italian wanted to learn how to sky dive. He got an instructor and started lessons. The instructor told the Italian to jump out of the plane and pull his rip cord. The instructor then explained that he himself would jump out right behind him so that they would go down together. The Italian understood and was ready.

The time came to have the Italian jump from the air plane. The instructor reminded the Italian that he would be right behind him. The Italian proceeded to jump from the plane and after being in the air for a few seconds pulled the rip cord. The instructor followed by jumping from the plane. The instructor pulled his rip cord but the parachute
did not open. The instructor, frantically trying to get his parachute
open, darted past the Italian.

The Italian seeing this yelled, as he undid the straps to his parachute, "So you wanna race, eh?"

Everyone has seen the 'clip pins' which pull out of the
fire extinguisher heads, and they look sort of like a grenade clip.
We yelled to our co-worker Jack, who was in the next room
"Hey Jack, how do you know when a Italian Terrorist is in
the area" and he responded 'I dunno'..."
At that point we threw three of the clips around the corner.

A popular bar had a new robotic bartender installed. A guy came in for a drink and the robot asked him, "What's your IQ?"
The man replied, "130." So the robot proceeded to make conversation about physics, astronomy, and so on. The man

listened intently and thought, "This is really cool."

Another guy came in for a drink and the robot asked him, "What's your IQ?" The man responded, "120." So the robot started talking about the Super Bowl, dirt bikes, and so on. The man thought to himself, "Wow, this is really cool." A third guy came in to the bar. As with the others, the robot asked him, "What's your IQ?" The man replied, "80." The robot then said, "So, how are things in Italy these days?"

The three latest Italian technological discoveries:
   1.) Solar powered flashlights
   2.) Inflatable dart boards
   3.) Helicopter ejection seats

Two Italian truck drivers are barreling along when they come up to an overpass. A sign says, "Clearance: 11"2'." So they get out, measure their truck, and realize that it's 11"6'. So the first Italian looks at the second Italian and says, "I don't see any cops around...let's go for it!"

An Italian was doing some experiments, teaching a frog to jump.
The training went on for a while and finally when he said, "Jump!" the frog will jump high in the air. He thought it was time to take some measurements and publish the results.

He started his measurements with
some twine, a ruler and a
knife. He placed the frog on a
wooden cutting plate and said,
"Jump."
It jumped and he measured the
height it jumped. He wrote
in his observation notebook:
"Height jumped (with 4 legs):
14 inches. Inference: None."
Then he cut one of the legs off the
frog and said, "Jump."
It jumped to a height of 10 inches.
Inference: None.
Then he cut the next leg, and
measured the height jumped.
Because it had only 2 legs the
height jumped was only 5 inches.
Then he cut one more leg and the
frog now had only one leg.

The height jumped was just 1 inch with one leg. Again the inference was none.
Then he cut the last leg off the frog and said "Jump!"
It didn't move at all. He wrote his inference in the
notebook: "When we removed all four legs, it turned deaf!"

Three prisoners, an American, a German, and a Italian, are scheduled to be executed by firing squad. They bring out the American and stand him in front of the Italian. He points and shouts, "Tornado!" They all look and the American runs away.
Next, they place the German in front of the firing squad. He yells

"Earthquake!" They all hit the dust and the German escapes.
Next up is the Italian. He looks around and shouts "Fire!"

This Italian came home one day from work, hung up his coat, took off his hat and walked into his bedroom shouting "honey I am home!"
What should he see but his best friend in bed with his wife.
Infuriated, he rushed to the cupboard, pulled out his gun and put it
to his head. His wife started laughing.
"Don't laugh!" he screams. "You're next!"

"This is eerie," replies the other, "I'm Welesa Tech, '81. Let's get another shot." But the bartender says, "Slow down fellas, I gotta make a call."
The bartender calls his wife and tells her that he'll be late getting home. When she inquires as to the cause, he replies, "Oh, the friggin' Liszjewski twins are here again."

"Wanna hear a great Italian joke?"
"Hey. I'm Italian!"
"Okay, I'll yell it slowly."

Italy sent its top team of scientists to attend the international science convention, where all the countries of the world gathered to compare their scientific achievements and plans. The scientists listened to the

United States describe how they were another step closer to a cure for cancer, and the Russians were preparing a space ship to go to Saturn, and Germany was inventing a car that runs on water. Soon, it was the Italian scientists' turn to speak. "Well, we are preparing a space ship to fly to the sun." This, of course was met with much ridicule. They were asked how they planned to deal with the sun's extreme heat. "Simple, we're going at night!"

One day a Italian father decides to take his son ice fishing.
So they head out onto the ice with all their gear and they
find a nice spot. So the father takes out his pickaxe and

starts chipping away.

They hear a loud, booming voice say, "THERE ARE NO FISH HERE!"

The father, astonished, looks at his boy and says, "Hear that? It's the fish gods!"

So they move a little ways down the ice and start digging again. Soon they hear the voice again, "THERE ARE NO FISH HERE!"

The father says to his son, "See? The fish gods are being good to us - we should move to find the fish."

So they move a little way down the ice again and, once more, start digging.

The voice booms once more,
"THIS IS THE RINK MANAGER.
THERE
ARE NO FISH HERE!"

Three men were all applying for the same job as a detective. One was Italian, one was Jewish, and one was Italian. Rather than ask the standard questions during the interview, the chief decided to ask each applicant just one question and base his decision upon that answer.
When the Jewish man arrived for his interview, the chief asked, "Who killed Jesus Christ?" The Jewish man answered without hesitation "The Romans killed him." The chief thanked him and he left.

When the Italian man arrived for his interview, the chief asked the same question. He replied "Jesus was killed by the Jews." Again, the chief thanked the man who then left.

When the Italian man arrived for his interview, he was asked the exact same question. He thought for a long time, before saying, "Could I have some time to think about it?" The chief said, "OK, but get back to me tomorrow." When the Italian man arrived home, his wife asked "How did the interview go?" He replied, "Great, I got the job, and I'm already investigating a murder!"

Three men want make phone call from Hell to remind to their

relatives about its harsh conditions Their nationalities were American, Italian and Italian. So they decide to go to Devil who is the boss. So the American made a call and the Devil made him to pay 100 USD, then an Italian made a call and the Devil made him to pay 10 Euros on fact that Italy is less developed than the USA. Lastly the Italian man made a call and the Devil made him to pay a cent Both the American and Italian complain as it is not fair and the devil responded to them "The Italian call was a local call whereas yours were international calls."

Two guys are in a bar, a small one and a big one. The small

one says to the big one: "Hey, wanna hear a dumb Italian joke?" "Sure," says the big, strong guy, "but I'll have you know I'm Italian. And so are they." The big guy motions toward two even bigger guys, who come over to the table. "They are my brothers."
One of the two brothers motions toward a bunch of other big Italian people who come over and introduce themselves as the cousins of the brothers of the big Italian guy. In the end there are about 20 HUGE Italian guys on the other side of the bar.
"So, so you STILL wanna tell that joke?" asks the big Italian guy.

"No," replies the small guy.
"Why not?" askes the big Italian guy, "scared?"
"Nope," replies the small guy, "I just don't feel like explaining it 5 times."

Knock Knock
Who's there?
Italy! Italy who?
Italy (it will be) all over in the morning.

Knock Knock
Who's there?
Rome!
Rome who?
Rome is where the heart is!

Knock Knock
Who's there?
Venice.
Venice who?
Venice your mom getting home?

An Italian guy goes to the doctor
and says, "Doctor, can you give me
a lobotomy?"
The doctor says, "Why on earth
would you want a lobotomy?"
The Italian responds, "Why, so I
can write 'dumb Italian' jokes, of
course!"

I once had a frightening encounter
in a bar in Alabama
over Italian jokes. I was with a
friend who I didn't
realize got mouthy when he drank.
He started telling

Italian jokes. I tried to silence him
because I was afraid
he would offend someone. Sure
enough, before I could shut
him up, a very large, very drunk
man walked to our table
and explained he was Italian and
was proud of his heritage
and did not like the jokes.
The bouncer saw what was
happening and made the man
leave. After about 20 minutes I
decided it was time to
get my friend out of there. As I
was trying to unlock
my car door in the parking lot I
heard a voice behind me
say, "I've been waiting for you sons
of bitches."
When I turned around the man was
behind me with a razor

in his hand. You cannot begin to
imagine the relief I felt
when I realized he didn't have any
place to plug it in.

Other books in this series:

Obnoxious Italian Jokes
Obnoxious Polish Jokes
Obnoxious Black Jokes
Obnoxious Gay Jokes
Lesbian Laughs
The Rabbi Joke Book
The Jewish American Princess
      Joke Book
The Not Quite Kosher Jewish
      Joke Book

Made in the USA
Coppell, TX
12 June 2023

18004213R00075